SOLAR
PROMINENCE

SOLAR
PROMINENCE

KEVIN CRAFT

Cloudbank Books

First Edition

Library of Congress Cataloging in Publication Data

Kevin Craft, 1967 —
        Solar prominence

ISBN: 0-9665018-9-6

Library of Congress Control Number:
        2005932820

Cloudbank Books is an imprint of

Bedbug Press
P.O. Box 39
Brownsville, OR 97327
www.bedbugpress.com

Cover photography from Getty Images/NASA TRACE
Cover design and book design by Brandon Conn
Cloudbank Books logo is a carving by Julie Hagan Bloch from
Haunting Us With His Love by David Samuel Bloch.
Text set in Bookman
Printed at Thomson-Shore, Inc., Dexter, Michigan

for Anaïs
daughter, firstborn, love

CONTENTS

⊙

◉◯

Acknowledgments

It was part of the colossal sun,

Surrounded by its choral rings,
Still far away.

—Wallace Stevens

TWO RAVENS

We circled each other,
trading pinnacles and views.
I scrambled up to where they
simply lifted off,
I threw an apple core into the wide
windy space beneath us:
neither one flinched, neither
moved an inch as it fell
out of sight—the used-up free-
fallen apple of my eye.
If they blinked, I couldn't see it—
black eye in black socket—
radiant black, black hole black.
And wings like liquid basalt.
They looked like rooks,
like any old crow,
except when they were close enough
to call to—perched on a rock
like pure exaggeration.
Hydraulic press, I thought.
Kettle and reticent pot.
What they thought of me
they kept to themselves—
not one squawk, not one dire utterance—
though by their dark demeanor
I gathered I was something
of a disappointment—
a scavenged picnic, a bone picked clean.
Or maybe they saw through
the point I climbed up to—
winded, heart beating hard—
and like the living daylight's negative
took the measure of darkness
there, left me to scribble
in my own black book.

SOPA DE PINTAS NEGRAS

Night dense with matter,
night of the ladle, salt & spoon
simmering on your blue flame,
night of the onion,
of the translucent stars—

break bread with me.
Break bread, as they once said—
those travelers wanting company
at a meal, a companion

for the road. Sit at my table,
one would beckon—a loaf before him,
a handful of crumbs on the floor—

sit down and I'll recount for you
the famished history of my flesh.

JANUS-INGENUOUS

January begets journey.
One day is a blue pedestal,
another rushes to meet you
off the ferry with a room to let.

You wouldn't know it
except by the smell of coriander
and the Statue of One Arm
marking the crossroad. Shade

begets shore. Two horn
blasts in the slack water harbor:
arrivals by the bundle,
a packet of farewells.

Only the old, on their mules, stay put.
Or the merchant in the market
weighing mint sprigs green
as the universe seen from a distance.

Or is that latte-beige? Three or four
faces you recognize
but from where? Tomatoes stewing
in their warm red skins.

Forget the annals, the tried tribunes.
Reason is a janitor at the back door
smoking. Yours is the blue door
with the lintel of meat.

There is laundry everywhere
hanging from windows, third
and fourth generation.
Ash begets lather, suds in the harbor.

There are things you should never
forget: God
is a strong detergent.
Look both ways when crossing a sea.

THE DIFFERENCE

He was a specialist of the early
hours, the fives and sixes a.m.
The gray mists, the newsprint, the red-eye's
surly flight path through the dream

lives of a city only half-awake:
he was an adept of daylight's darkness
beginning to depart in blues
behind the mountains, in flowers arched

over the disorienting desert,
in dewy windshields and rear view
mirrors, a leading edge of red
the spillover from stupendous noon

in the Azores, siesta in Sicilia
spouting tropospheric plumes of ash and loess.
His thesis was terminal restlessness—
cloudy islands and theatrical volcanoes,

bays groomed by canoes and circled by float planes,
the migratory stunts of coho and flycatchers,
a small brown estuary
in the saucer on his table. The stature

of cypresses, like gaunt ministers
in shadow governments, made him think twice
about standing for office.
But could he be in two places at once,

divide his time between zones
and pocket the difference... There's heed
he thought, in clockwork, in going always hence.
The earlier he'd wake, the further east

he found himself, fitting out scales
with blood oranges, preparing to duel
by a misty river, deciphering dust
in a cuneiform wedge. Was it hope for renewal,

the way a dream could dawn on high drama,
drawing semi-circular crowds?
Tragedy plays throughout the morning, backed
by a chorus of stationary shrouds.

And beyond the pale, where a gallery
tunnels into its metamorphic hill,
the rows of like-minded dead choosing sides
like flowerbeds on a window sill.

TOULOUSE

Arriving at each new city, the traveler
finds again a past of his
that he did not know he had...
                    —Calvino, *Invisible Cities*

1

Toulouse in February is the clarity of brick:
such a spring-ready sun on the muddy Garonne,
all the fresh red faces drawn
out-of-doors. Echoes of a clarinet deepen
under arches of the Pont Neuf where even
the dogs are dressed for a picnic:
Toulouse is February's clarity of brick.

2

Toulouse in March is the bluster of glass—
sunlight stained and narrowed in the tall
windows of the Jacobins, late-blooming mural
of a murky afternoon.
Now Thomas Aquinas, asleep in the stone,
is dreaming up uses for an imperfect past—
Toulouse in March is the luster of glass.

3

Toulouse in April is fonder of marble,
pink-veined, non-plussed, the dreaming blood
frozen in an emperor's head.
Civil servants appear with the day's wage
on the square, their grievances aging
in smoke and beer as the music ungarbles,
Toulouse in April is fond of its marble.

4
Come May Toulouse is the frailty of steel:
behind scaffolding, painstakingly restored,
the hôtel façades Cocagne adored
rise with the fortunes of the pastel princes.
They stroll the arcades, gleaning by glimpses
the country no commerce can turn to pure zeal:
Toulouse in May is frailty in steel.

STEEPLEJACK

My steeplejack grandfather dangles
from the blackened lip of a spent smokestack
rising above the factories of south Philly,
lunch strapped in a pail to his waist.
He is up pointing fissures
in the brickwork again, each new day

the rope-and-pulley scramble into place,
alone or in pairs, bronze skin blazing
in the fetid air. Below, the widening
depression of the Delaware sends its ships
to sea; Camden burns on the far shore.
My steeplejack grandfather brings

his full weight to bear on the rope,
swings around the hollow shell of fumes
to test each heat-scarred inch of mortar.
He is just twenty and this is fine work,
poised above the city's slattern yards.
If he slips the knot holding him, leans

a little farther out into the bright haze
ghosting the low outlines of buildings,
he can hear the war coming
that sweeps him off to Seattle, Honolulu,
one far-flung atoll to the next, though he seems,
for now at least, unfazed:

what is it to exchange one rope
for another, dropped from the open
belly of a plane to dangle from a chute's taut ends?
He is still among those a wind will spare,
spiraling down in the shell-blackened
telltale taste of fire in his throat.

W.B.V. 1917 - 1998

CAFÉ DU SOLEIL

It can't be helped. Where a canal divides
the dry brickwork of the city, and water,
bottle-green, stalls, thinning to a trickle

over rocks, it can't be helped. Where crowds
press beneath bright awnings leaning down
a long avenue of darkened windows

whose shadows buttress the terra cotta
weight of roofs on which the heat
sprawls out to sleep, still it can't be helped.

Romanesque in sunlight, a row of palms
is whittled down to little more than a limp
shade scuffling among so many blades

of grass, and who can help it? The Romans
have left their towns in ruin, their priests
to haggle over demographics.

Even the troubadours have found that love falters.
And who among us sitting here remembers
now the stinging intimacy of rain

except these waiters, white-apron cool, who thread
the makeshift sidewalk aisles, tilting
trays of cocktails over unbowed heads?

INCENSE

Pungent filament,
      finespun swirling line hung
in air, snaring
      nothing in particular, conspicuous
as a live wire nonetheless:
      how incense
holds sway,
      climbing the narrow chimney of itself
only to
      come undone
at the fluent end
      of its dominion,
giddy as a silkworm gone
      sensationally astray. Here
is the frayed rope charmed out of ash,
      here the nimble
melody of the flute—
      featherweight, aria
of aroma, the air's own
     nom de plume.
Who will trace
    this signature of smolder, who translate
the nomenclature of smell
     as it permeates a room,
path of the supplicant's unhurried prayer?
     Nothing if not
sweet time—sandalwood, scent
      of green mountains, of the redolent
middle of spring—time
     raveling in the deepest sense,
the amnesiac season
      growing fragrant, accountable, as it burns
down the length of its fuse.

FIN DE SIÈCLE

The sundial reads *it's later than you think.*
Black humor of the dark ages going blind.
The sowers are asleep again by noon.

Meanwhile, sunlight saturates the brickwork
of the Palace of the Kings, gets in eyes
like grit kicked up by an unkind wind.

In the palm-studded cool of the courtyard
the King raises a glass to his guests,
the Duke and Archbishop of Languedoc.

His sovereignty's at stake, and the bread
is stale. What can he do but serve them
lemonade? If this heat keeps up the rapeseed

will wilt in the fields. No wonder then
the painter's brushstrokes all approximate
the grainy interior of the sun-

flower: so many faces turned his way
at once, their slender shadows decomposed
in the soil. The King declares a holiday.

The field hands know it's later than you think.

IN LIEU OF AN ODE

I would like to feed my indolence
to the fire in the stove
which would eat it up greedily
then sniff about smartly

for more. Because a dog knows
there's always more where that came from,
especially if it has to wait
all night at the porch door

with a dirty water dish.
I shift a little in my seat, turn
a few pages in a book
and already I can feel the day

going nowhere, spinning its wheels,
and the dog outside
yelping furiously at strangers who
look on bemusedly

as it chases its own black tail.
O for a muse of fire
begins the tale of bright invention,
and who wouldn't on occasion

love to see a bush in the yard
burst into flame? To be sure,
the azaleas put up a good show
each spring—such gaudy

pyrotechnics—but they have
only so much up their sleeves.
Dead of winter, days of summer—
perhaps you too have felt this way—

I'd settle for a ready game of fetch
or, better yet, a table for two
at *Il Forno di Luigi,* whose gnocchi
is out of this world.

THE PANTHEON (1)

Planetary altitudes, a concrete
coffered heaven, crowning oculus
blank as the zero no Roman ever knew
by which daylight enters—circumscribed, filled—
as cleanly as it passes through the dark
dilated upcast pupil of the eye;
where stars appear and drift in minute arcs
or capital clouds rain fluted columns;

where, as Helios climbs toward high noon
a pale, projected, second sun declines:
bright monocle, this hindsight, retinal
backlog, like the fixed gaze of a fallen god
who feels an image scattered, inverted
in the warm marble temple of his mind.

UMBRELLA PINES

Or, as the 19th century preferred,
Parasol—: one raised up in sun, bright side
of the coin, forge and bristling shield;
the other, diminutive *umbra*, eclipsing

moon's cuffed sleeve sweeping the planet
parish by parish, the day's undoing
in a glory of shade. Chiaroscuro lovely
and singular on hills, staked to their own

ground zero—daydream's burled and braided
halo, *haut-lieu* of the afternoon nap.
They grow tall, resilient, balancing
their unburdened sway like bindles,

or like the taut wrist and splayed fingers
beneath a clean-cut waiter's tray,
stern as silhouettes, cultivating carefree airs
as if they had somewhere else to get to

and all the time in the world.
Which may be why Cézanne
places one in high relief against the mottled sun-
struck Provençal plain it overlooks

so plainly, bystander and cynosure both,
so etched into foreground it extends
as much patchwork field before it
as behind. The dirt lane that winds

diagonally through the middle distance
toward the gravityless, violet-gray edifice
of Mont Sainte-Victoire becomes another
branch leading the viewer in—slender,

an indistinguishable hay-deepened dwindling
down which an old woman wanders,
almost a stoop-shouldered shadow herself.
Or why on the Palatine, resolute amid ruins,

they draw the tiered and toppled city to them,
ascending the awkward strata
centuries make of streets, road upon road
and way upon way straddling plunder,

a peaceable pasture grazed to brick
and broken marble, civic sediment,
subsuming myth. They hold
the hill in place, bring footloose

to a standstill—each an interior,
a pole-vaulted bay self-possessed
at the height of exposé, the watchful
green sprawl of sunlight propped open over

its sovereign, homespun underworld, that Rome
built and dismantled each day.

AFTER A JOURNEY

Sous le pont d'Avignon,
on y danse, on y danse...

You wake, as you sometimes do,
in the middle of a moonless night.
Now where has the errant bird dropped you?
Where might your ship put in?

You've no idea
where you are
a long disquieting
minute or two until

a bloodless arm unbends at your side
and you can pick out of darkness
the contours of your own bedroom....

*

I make a little pile
of stones I've picked up there & here—
my *hermeia*, ambit cairn
of touchstone souvenirs—
agate, jasper, meteorite, carnelian,
each enamored of a mile.

*

Xenon—Greek guestroom—
though joined to the main house,
always a separate entrance.
Goes to show how
a traveler grows
intimate with estrangement.

*

Of necessity, travelers in antiquity
made certain to arrive before daylight expired.

To *journey* is to make a day of it,
to find dailiness sufficient, the mundane divine.

*

Garden of string beans
and overgrown balconies—
each thing wants its up
and away. Would settle for
a little survey
and domain, some home
to call tomorrow—*à demain,
Cher Chez!
Vous cherchez encore? Adieu!*

*

Marooned in the Tiber, a ruined bridge:
flash flood, immemorial invasion.
Ponte Rotto—broken instep, stone half
skipped, half sunk, relentlessly between.

*

On their roads, the Romans
invented the summer vacation.
Driven by heat, they'd retreat
to cool hill- or sea-side villas,
up with the dawn, Colli Albani,
down to dusk-stark Capri,
carving peristyles out of mid-day,
vacating the stifling plain.

Vacancy: becoming an absence—
veluti in speculum, ventis secundis—
to veer between voyage and void—

*

like the young goatherd *en vacances*
in busy Avignon. High season:
for a week he stays
in the hostel room, venturing
no farther than the balcony,
napping afternoons while reading—*vade*
mecum—*Around the World in 80 Days.*

*

About the time it takes
Cavallini to complete *The Last Judgment*
in medieval Santa Cecilia, perhaps, *giornata*
per giornata, the day's plaster
dried out by supper, colorfast,
a pastel rippling of robes, rounded jaws
and rainbow wings, an upraised hand
on the threshold of displacement....

*

Zeno's paradox: a journey
of infinite half-steps
never ends. Stop-
motion: at any given instant
a loosed arrow
stills. Nothing moves.
The runner
in the Circus Maximus
is heading for a photo-finish.

*

The linear journey, the itinerary, the trip
from A to B, before and after, is only
the apparent journey. So many dodges,
feints, errands, forays, and excursions,
so many detours and delays,
so much backpedaling, lingering, retracing
of steps, side trips, respite, aimless arcing,
racing ahead... To move by the calendar's
lunacy: first the death, then the dying,
then the dear departure.

*

And so long goodbyes.

*

Because Hermes loves
both travelers and thieves,
Petrarch, laurel-wreathed,
leaving beloved Rome
after a first and long-awaited visit,
is accosted by bandits
and robbed. 1341:
the city slumps behind him
in splendid disrepair.

Forced to turn back
for an armed escort,
he sees those gates only
once thereafter, passing
the rest of his life in the north
moving from city to city, *solo
e pensoso*, in various *cameretti*
composing his praises
to the point of no return.

*

Summer is an archer flush with arrows.
The sky is charged with hospitality.
Forlorn hope is a lost expedition.

*

Vintner from vine,
horseman from hay—

Sous le pont d'Avignon
on y danse, on y danse...

since 1635 when
floods swept half of it away.

*

A week home now, bags
still unpacked, as if to finish the job
would seal my end—
death indivisible, the disbelieving
pose of paradox resolved—

*

The story is restoration, sing-along,
in millennial Avignon: the city plans
to rebuild its bridge's famous, missing
spans, only to tear them down again
the following year. At what cost? A song.

TO ERR

It was the era
of ore, of ages ago,
of alps scored by ice
and ill-winds.

It was a Monday
when the month began,
better late
than larvae, better now

than law—it was the eve
of ere too long.
It was what it was,
what it always was,

the aye and awl of it,
the awful arc, the airs.
And yet: I was all ears
beside the sea, mud

in your eye, I was out
of my mind in yon.
It was the era
of *ore*, of italic hours,

walking about
too many urns for a sun.
You were your own
worst enemy, I

the odd one out, ages
of ash ago,
and smoking alps,
and alms.

IMPRESSIONISM

On the first day they mowed
the waist-high meadow down.

I took my hands from my sleeves
to walk out into the beaten field.

It was like doing handstands
on a thatched cottage roof

in medieval Languedoc.
A few coins slipped from my pockets—

and confetti, a blank note
someone had drawn

a crisp fedora on: all posy
sifting down through the straw.

I could hear the soft
cries of women huddled around

black kettles. I could hear
rats chewing into the wood.

Over the yellow hill, the rattling
of trundles, and wheel-ruts

trembling with dust.
On the first day they mowed

the waist-high meadow down
it was like looking through a haystack

with the heart crossed, one hand
tied behind the back.

And then the hopeless pact to die.
I walked out into the beaten field,

barely a flicker
in the needle's eye.

BAGGAGE

Outside the glass the season's turning—
yellow sun on a red tile roof, black grapes
in fat rows beyond the tracks. Barely

time to think, decide—a woman
in polyester flower print presses through
a turnstile, scuttles down the quay, suitcase

yelping at her heels: passing
one door then another she settles
on a third—non-smoking, second class—

and helps her halting bag up
narrow stairs, waving past a window as the shrill
whistle scatters pigeons to the tiles.

THE PANTHEON (2)

Planetarium of vague influences,
pinpoint dispositions, broad blue daylight

deified: where a dome establishes
eminent domain, sky predominates.

And the vagaries of sky: clouds, gulls, clues.
A niche for each of seven sojourners
in heaven, divine motives, mundane moods.

Though doomsday come, let *jovial* prevail
beside those junior joys, mercurial, fleet,
in contemplation's pale.
                Here light translates
lust into a swan, a swoon from golden rain:
and so we're fooled, our fame diurnal.

Let every dog on earth have his
though livelong burn through heads and high acclaim.

12/21

When no more bound
to huddle and hone,
take care
dear crony, prone to carrion
extravagance.
Whistle through a bone.

Nothing save
passage where scope
is feeling, azimuth
throws up its arms.
To astronomers tabling
coffee—long shifts
and backaches, Arabia mapped
by guzzle and regard.

Can you feel the full moon
down your neck, aftermath?
Its pallor stalks
the grassy lot.
O positive void,
cold enough fear
is near enough solace—
that compassing darkness
takes us in. Down
and out we go again.

From now, all's salvo
and alarm.

BIRCHES

Not for purity or for pedigree or
the way the morning becomes their shining
example, these birches on the edge of clearings
that meadows make among hemlock and black pine—

so slender their brightness startles, thinning
the air like a hot filament. Of course
it helps, dead of winter, to have magnitudes
of snow thrown about them in all directions,

wide-eyed sky-empty snow not so much
erasure as an excavation of air that birches
tunnel out of like reckless moles
tapering to a stand-up pinpoint invisibility—

white lightning bolted fast, the rawest nerves—
matter and fact—exposed, all ganglia
and leaping synapse as the season lapses
storm by watch, blizzard yard by thaw. If they fail

it's all at once, upended by gale, collapsed
in a heap of sweet stove wood, salmon-pink
beneath the wrinkled bark, almost tender,
but I never saw it. All winter they held

the light the way a window does, basking
in transparency, a glazier's dream house
blueprint for building from the sky down.
And in spring, flecked thigh-high with mud,

they drip like parchment salvaged from a flood,
peeling scroll and runic scar, illuminated
manuscripts copied out line for lacuna
to make a ragtag love of disbelief.

MEDICAL HISTORY

If the body is eighty
percent water, a man
might drown simply lying
down to sleep, or walking
to the corner store
for bread and a newspaper
find himself struggling to stay afloat
in the riptide of his own bad blood.

Cars racing down the street
trying to beat that mistimed
series of red lights come
screeching to a halt, but no one can save him
as he steps from the curb into the rain-
swollen river of himself
swept under, found some three weeks
later face down in a salty marsh
where river spills into the bay.
Papers run the story
with obsequious headlines
and a thumb-sized portrait
fished from his high school yearbook.

Half sleeping or half awake,
is it not the same face that rises out of froth
and a ring of black stubble, tepid mornings
by the porcelain sink
where steam on the mirror
is a second skin, the permeable membrane
riddled with soft light?
Is the body, then, twenty percent
glare, the refracted splendor of a few bright ideas
stuck like light bulbs in the plaster ceiling?

The first time my father's heart
nearly failed, they repaired it by dragging
a balloon through his chest.
He said the light in the hospital
room made him dizzy. For months he took pills
to thin out his blood. One summer—
I must have been
ten or eleven—we sat all day
in a rowboat fishing,
trolling the brackish estuary of Egg Harbor River
for perch and pike. I didn't like fishing as much
as being out on the water
with him so obviously in his element,
content in his thick tan skin.

I caught nothing.
Whatever he caught he threw back.
To tease me he liked to rock the boat from side to side
or stand up abruptly in its shallow middle
and feign falling backwards—arms flailing,
face a comical O—all but promising
to spill us both
into its sun-speckled wake.

GONE WEST

We were in the Badlands
remembering the good times.

We were in the Black Hills
when the black mood struck.

In the Country of Nothing
Between Us, a magpie.

Coyotes yelping at the horizontal sun.
I tried to take the sagebrush

at its word. You followed
the divining rod

to the canyon's edge.
On far ridges,

the great white micro-
wave drums were beating.

Magpies flaunting clownish masks.
You told me the legend

of the hanging valley.
I sang the ditty

of the wandering ford.
This must be the place, I ventured.

Now to cross Dry Creek
without claiming our reward.

AN OLIVE

An olive's self-knowledge is complicated
by years of standing apart, rooted in rocky,
drought-prone ground, an ingrown go-it-alone
ethic in the twisted trunk-braids hunched
beneath scant leaves, tethered to a flickering
hive of shade. Even in a grove it is self-involved,
bent upon some puzzlement the Stoics
abandoned long ago, hard-nosed, opaque,
working the problem over until a stubborn fruit comes,
the green-gold oil drummed from stone....

An Andalusian friend once told me about an olive
that saved his life, the only shelter in a bull pasture
he'd stumbled into unawares walking down
from Grazalema. He saw the stocky wind-snare
crouched on a mound of loam and aimed for it,
the one landmark in a dry expanse, self-evident,
splendid in isolation when, a stone's throw farther off,
he caught sight of a bull grazing in a weedy ravine.
He froze. The day went white, he said, his body
cold with sweat, beads of it budding on his lip.
And then the bull spotted him.

As it wheeled to face him like a great
weather vane, snorting in complaint,
Antonio sidled toward the tangled hutch—
his compact hope, his city-state of loam and leaves
and meticulous, hard-won fruit—
trying to make himself, limb by limb, its green citizen.
But the bull stood its offish ground, intransigent,
placid, until night fell and the yellow village lights
appeared on the hillcrest. Antonio likewise,
though numb with appeasement—stuck there, he said,
until the virgin led him away.

ASCETICISM

I like the way Jerome
presses his thumb
into the crease of the Vulgate
in El Greco's *St. Jerome.*
I like the way his thumb,
the opposable thumb of Jerome,
is long and thin and pointed
like his face, his somber face,
gaunt and elongated
by a hanging cloud of beard.
Too, his straight
and narrow nose, slightly
twisted at the tip,
is a prominence to behold,
a formidable distance
from which to look
a long way down,
the sometime Roman
nose of St. Jerome. And if
his cheek is chiseled
out of ambient dark,
and if his mouth is pursed
and droops at the corners,
and if his gaze drifts
sidelong past the painter—
master of the vertical
composition—to the pale
familiar waiting elsewhere
in the room, still the thumb
is a staff, the weight
enough to hold his place
on the page, a pillar even
on which to rest
his body's nimble ruin.

MY CLONE

frowns when he finds out he's not alone.
Was grown from cells
scraped from the inside of my cheek.
I'm nobody's second string,

he insists to the talk show host
egging us on. (Loud applause
from the studio audience.) I'm a self-
made man, not the other

way around. Steely-eyed and neatly
groomed, he's as brash
as a dressing room mirror.
Backstage he takes me aside.

Nothing personal, he admits, running a hand
through his long black hair.
They put us on to air our differences,
is all. Thought I'd play ball.

He does, in fact, play soccer
in the Italian leagues.
He was shipped at cell's first division
to a western fertility lab,

so that we grew up on opposite coasts, a case
of nurture versus second
nature. He is savvy
beyond his years and makes me seem

thwarted and unsure. And now he sniffs
the guestroom cabernet, smoking a fat cigar.
Is this what it means to turn the other cheek?
Perhaps, he says, stretching

out on the double bed as if
he counts the same sheep I do before sleep
or reads the Dadaists for moral instruction.
As for second guessing, he adds,

you're not the only one.

METAL-LITURGICAL

Maine is the sculptor's state—
the old blocking shoulder chipped and crumbling,
socket for a crow's storm-broken wing.

That bearded coast, incessant
termite ocean tunneling into slender headlands,
that take-it-on-the-chin

peninsular parry and thrust.
And the archipelago drift of ellipsis, day
after day, school of hard knocks and nails.

Nails: tendon and ligament, stigmata
and polish. The sculptor's stainless
steel garden a bed to lie down on—

flowering field or barbed wire cloud—
a bed to climb out of unscathed. And so a feat
like acupuncture or vaccination—

the wound applied to ward off greater harm,
a wilderness of self-immolation
gloved hands bend into unhammered shape.

SEASTACKS

Like outposts
of the continent, stepping
stones to somewhere cloud-bound
or disappearing with the tide,

the sea besieging
and the siege called off.
A thousand birds
nest on ledges—tufted

puffins, storm petrels,
guillemots and gulls
niched in seagrass
and guano, guileless

before unsteady weather,
exiles of the credible shore.
Every inch
rising from the tide

is evidence of the living rock:
beneath the waterline
anemones mouth
the surf, barnacle colonies

pop and hiss, starfish
wedge into each fissure,
wrap each boss
in a thick embrace.

Bulkheads of the headland,
plinth and pediment,
grand arch excavated
wave by wave:

how they stagger out of froth,
standoffish, grave,
where the two of us
hold out for more.

TO AN AMPHORA, SALVAGED @

Emptied amplitude, sunk by storm or some
blunder of the rudder in fog, the oils
and wines poured from your torso too late
to appease the cross, sullen god of seas,

or leaked back slowly over centuries
to kelp, coral, the seafloor's cold, dreamless
pastoral; fortune's orphan, amputee...
It's like awkward, untried luck to see you

standing on one stout foot—up like a top,
iron-girdled, like a voluminous
mollusk, if far more shapely. And not
my luck alone—old Attic trophy shouldered

home from the meet, a victor's spoil—larger
than life or hunched and fetal, belly enough
to climb into except for the undilated neck.
You are everywhere in these latitudes

something to behold, muraled in Egyptian
tombs, half-buried in Etruscan silt, antique honey
perfectly preserved. And where luck stayed true,
arranged in careful Punic storehouse rows,

or built up into a discarded hill
in Testaccio where the outcasts are buried,
or here, more commonly, you take your bearings
from rooms of a Franciscan monastery

which doubles as a maritime museum
in Hvar. How far, in that once upon a time
province of Illyria—where Diocletian
retired after dividing the empire

and many fledgling Christians from their souls,
where shipwrecked Viola washed ashore
and found her lover's love in mourning cruel,
so stood beside the surf, a servant's ruse,

doubly pleading for her waterlogged twin,
where Venetian traders found lavender
to their liking, and pellucid light, stone
the color of cappuccino foam, where

perhaps (who knows better than you, unflagging
decanter of Adriatic languor)
the famous duplicitous wanderer
of whale-roads and unsafe harbors himself

found ten years' solace in sorcery's embrace
a mere stone's throw from home—how far here
from hallmark wheel and kiln? Long
before the hourglass had turned slow time

into a sand dune, amorphous mirror image
of the undermining sea, you were trade's
eccentric tale, oblong apple of the sailor's eye
and so time's voluptuous capsule,

whose story is the salt-emblazoned glaze,
whose song is the swirl and rush of water
through bottlenecks and straits—Messina or
Gibraltar, the epiglottal Dardanelles—

wherever compression quickens the pulse
of navigation, as for the mariner
in whose mouth long vowels—*fo'c'sle, staysail*—
are swallowed back like pitch-hot retsina,

the mariner whose drowning is sorrow and euphoria
and the sea lanes stretched between them like pure
conjecture.... O to lie down in the whirlpool
of history and wake up, blank-eyed, blameless,

in the clearing of a throat, solvent as the riddle
anchored here: no longer attention's shapely
center, but its far-flung entrepôt, its worn-
about-the-neck pirate amulet

or drifter's dog-tag address, lost and found,
where anyone homesick or seasick hears
the choral bubbleburst of compact vowels
rehearsing echo-relocated awe

or resurfacing as an extravagant
disbeliever's *ah* fastened to a mast,
a storied preposition: and so you bear
what we can't (and even what we can: the monks

having long since ushered us few from the museum
and gone about their prayers)—all motion
ascribed to the heart's steady restlessness
but likely more akin to an electron's

struck from the shell of its whirlwind and spinning
out counterclockwise to the antic world,
the cipher sea, @ large again, a silence
speaking volumes, blinking now and then

like a cyclops whose godsent ship's come in.

DROWNING MAN

It's neither here nor there, once
upon a time in a blue moon perhaps.

I mean, days like these, perhaps
the grass is greener on the other hand,

perhaps not. I might make up my mind
by now if you care to hear me out.

I mean, I had this island once—
and in the meantime these ships.

And there I was, far and away
beyond the shadow of a doubt, not green

at all but blue in the face again
up talking all night with the sea—no,

it was the sea doing the talking,
I just had to shut up

and get a word in edgewise.
And it went on like that for months.

And in the meantime, these ships—
they came and went and what

could I do about it until one day
a plane and I all but died

laughing. I mean, days like these,
they're once in a blue moon.

No grass can grow here anyway,
if you get my drift.

And if you could see me now, head
over heels beyond the shadow

of a doubt, you'd know
there's no place on earth

I wouldn't meet you halfway.

CINQUETERRE

Pastel, pinafore vernacular—
linked like any dove-
lovely olive grove or lemon tree
to belfry and vertigo, color
to warm sea-lidded eyes.

HOMEBODY

Tea steeps.
Stones wait.
The status
quo evaporates
like pickets
on a fence.
Only keeps
from going hence
those picaros
at the epileptic gate
dividing prescience
from pretense.

My time has come
and gone,
like a circus
before dawn.
Some say less
is more, others
more or less
derive their loneliness
from plenary session.
I launder
and I laminate.
Who wanders

from task to task
soon founds
a city-state.
One learns
not to mask
long questions.
One counts
on many returns—
as moss
profiles a maple,
as trade winds sop up
oceans ounce by ounce.

K

Sturdiest of consonants—oak of the forest,
clap of the hand, flying buttress

at the back of the throat. As upright
as a monk in a garden hoeing corn,

tending rows of new tomatoes, shoveling
dung in a cowshed done milking the cows

at dawn. Potash of flue dust
melted into glass. Salty cant of sailors

in the harbor at Tyre. Fulcrum,
pivot, ricochet—sheer

kinetic fury of hot gas—the big
bang in *kosmos*, silent prayer in *kneel.*

Kingmaker, capstone, coral reef,
sand bank where waves break in long lines

off the coast. Assurance in OK, swift
jab and black-out in KO.

In heaven, cumulus; kilometer on earth.
Worth its weight in gold, pearl, salt.

Clap of the hand, coldest of zeros:
slows the restless atom to a halt.

THE WEATHER IN HEAVEN

It's all they talk about in heaven, and why not?
On earth we think the weather
beneath our larger aspirations and call it

small talk—the chatter you hear at the fringes
of the party where no one knows
another and everyone is waiting for the band

to launch into the next set—small talk, as if
we could shrink the weather
down to size and pack it away in mason jars

huddled on a pantry shelf with the plum preserves,
the windfall, pared and pressed, of all
we'd hoped to say but didn't, or couldn't, who knows.

Not so in heaven, where the big news is the latest
blizzard to have dumped forty inches
in the streets and all the dead out together

breaking ice. Because they are forgetful and must
get reacquainted every day,
it's always snowing in heaven, or raining, or the sun

breaking majestically through clouds, and the dead
assemble in the square
like good citizens. Coffee is served in white cups

all day long. The dead in heaven know better
than to speak of angels
or utter promises when the rainbows reappear.

Instead they are content to mingle, say hello,
and fill their talk with such things
as they are—*mock sun, iceblink, window blind*—passing

word for fairer word into night.

YOUR NAME

is Anaïs—listen:
more than wind in trees,
more than sudden snow
in a field left overnight,
the body's light
is all rupture and blush
where the tips of capillaries
flare and a bruise
decorates your temple,
child of the unwielded knife
come slightly scathed into your life
and into one mother-
tongue or two: how
mine flutters the first time
I speak out your name,
rehearse each letter into rhyme
under my breath and love
that the thatch of vowels
in Anaïs kindles up suddenly,
a blaze teased
from the throat and cleaving
a small round shape
of its own in air.

AGAINST NECESSITY

Two seasons idle
in storage beneath the porch
and my red bike
is finally fixed—flat
tires inflated, brakes
tightened, hairpin trigger
of the derailleur repaired—
my red bike revived
like spring itself,
a pistol cleaned
and loaded, sudden
sunlight and a flair
for speed, windlass
hoisting wind, sprinter,
climber, faithful steed
of the asphalt plain—
my bike red-shifted
like a galaxy
racing outward
toward its beginning,
no end in sight, like a bend
in the road, like elbow
grease, the camber
gravity grinds out of space
or groove a gunshot
wears in time, the split-
second tear between
barrel and black,
gear and glide—my red
bike spinning wheels and a thread
so fine it can't be seen,
of fate or the failure
of nerve that separates
what is from what might
have been in a world
powered by pedal and chain.

PHILOLOGY

A few words find you in sleep:
luck, love, country, hunger, light.

They're your words, there. They move
you like a nimble herd

grazing the plain: love, dumb
luck, the vast country

they've barely crossed into, all appetite
and open range. Sawgrass,

saguaro, sugar pine, stream.
Wherever they go it's the same

snowy mountain draws near them
each night, the same glacial thaw

or rain, great river of runoff
thick with flour of their dead.

On the banks, a footprint. Higher
a hand painted red on rock, sleek

as an antelope. All appetite.
Every stone rising like bread.

OYSTERS

Settle in their beds of sizzle.
The breaded kind, pan-fried,
arrive in a dream of luxury,
pleasure boats dotting the bay.

Others come on the half-shell,
briny and tender as a wound,
the dollop of flesh
pried from its cloister,

succulent in its own secret spit.
To swallow one raw
and whole is like swallowing
your own tongue, or someone's,

the unspeakable savor of another
undone. Once, at The Ark,
we ordered plate after plate, then
drunk in the clear night air

climbed the chalk pale mound of shells
piled high as the roof
behind the steaming kitchen. There we sang
the song of all you can eat

which is the sharp-edged song
of bivalves and diphthongs
spilling their guts, split between joy
and the pitch black silence of the bay.

Night creaked against its moorings,
measureless. The night the mollusks made
their disheveled music,
we ate all there was to say.

CAN'T RECANT

You, my opposite, my sheer irresistible. Like hunters in a duck-blind, like gatherers up in arms. I might as if but no not yet: there are secrets and there are sofa-beds, and sometimes you must choose. Trim fingernails on the one hand, on the other let them grow. A larch in autumn is blatant contradiction, but football is a stupid sport. Still, there is no audience for featherweight, or so I thought. (Eavesdrop and you'll hear what's what.) So nice when you get tired and time for bed: some drowsy neighborhood you know, so dwell. Sleepwalk me through it: the Elysian for grandstanding, Coastal Kitchen for lure. Blind date no show, that's the life. I'd like to get away with it. How much future can one man take? One day at a time, that's the telemark technique, the switchback way down the vertical galore. Oh to be paramount, and mean it (gleaning heir apparently). The comic effect of speaking your mind in all situations: there's a fine line to laughter, good-bye. To wit, and otherwise save it for the afterlife. (Don't mention poverty, don't mention the soul). If you were I, if he were you... (If you think too much about it, fade). Larches know: they stand like spindly gold-leaf sponges taking all the moisture in. Mist and moisture, not seeing is believing. Believing is deciduous, contradiction letting go.

SLEEPING DOGS

Their legs all itch,
        paws scratching at
the warm pine floor
        which, to them, is a big wood

riddled with small wild game.
        They snarl and whine,
their breathing belabored,
        something they can't

quite catch. The strangers
        at the fence, the curious
stench of moldering crab
        curled up in a wet nostril,

low-tide, mud flat,
        an open stretch
of gull-speckled beach...
        Sometimes you want

to lie down with them,
        to brave the animal
kingdom come
        slumbering into the room,

hand to mouth,
        nose to the ground, the wind
a clean bone
        you thought was gone forever.

REUNION

We arrived from great distances
though none farther than the comet
wagging its eager tail at twilight.

All day long hot air balloons
set down easily in the grassy field
our many horses grazed,

tall ships moored in the lagoon.
Even the conventional
yellow taxis shuttling back

and forth between airstrip
and fairground were stunned
by our numbers, our elaborate

costumes, how we remembered
every name. As the tents went up
skywriters kept drafting vast

proposals in a gusty script until
a corps of new lovers was engaged.
By nightfall pavilions

blazed like fixed stars: magicians
and jugglers worked the crowds
with the usual tenpins and card tricks

while raconteurs held court center stage.
I remember loud music
and confetti, the girl who kissed me

at midnight by the punchbowl whispering
Happy New Year though clearly
it was summer because her skin

was tan. Then someone with broad
shoulders picked up an accordion
and began singing ballads by the bonfire

around which everyone drew near.
For hours we listened
or joined in as the song required

until even our empty bottles
hummed and whistled their last cheers.
Toward dawn the diehards

could still be heard laughing softly
as their marshmallows browned
or burned. It was ten

or twenty years before we'd see
the likes of it again, though in our lifetimes
the comet never returned.

LA STRADA LIGGIA

In the bay last night they went fishing by lamplight,
fifty boats, or more: they floated like candles
in a dusky chapel, each encased in the offshore dark.
Think of the anchovies glittering in their nets
like the torn out linings of deep-pocketed clouds.

Early this morning, the sky read storm.

The sea grew outlandish. It blasted the cliff
like a road-building crew. It was crass, it was pissed,
it was nobody's business. The inroads it made
hid the undocumented, migrants with fingernails
etched in salt.

Or so he tells me, the Professor of Vapors
pacing in the kitchen
two floors down. He was making a mess
of his tenth cappuccino, had kept
an all-night vigil at the foot of his bed.

When I joined him downstairs
he was clearly exhausted. Or maybe it was
just his way. I listened as he muttered
through warm foam, then left in a hurry without his
        papers.
I couldn't read them, though I tried—his hand
all nervousness and heavy sighs, like sky-writing,
monumental Aramaic.

I opted for a walk instead.
In the olive grove doves were cooing.
They didn't belong to any organized religion.
The path I was following
signified landslide. I walked as fast as I could uphill.

SOLAR PROMINENCE

There is a way the stars
figure in desire
but it's not what you think.
That one planet
or another winks out the night
you are born
means little anymore
though it used to be disaster.
Now when the sun
enters a house no one bothers
to pick up after it; the lease
is month to month.
Consider:
tenant to whichever sign
it throws the same
phantom weight around.
That's desire: the dark
which forms a rash as cooler
currents cross its face
marks the circuit crashing
end of one stupendous flame.
The sun doesn't mind.
It's never led a spotless life
to begin with.

ACKNOWLEDGMENTS

Many thanks to the editors of the journals in which these poems, some in earlier versions, first appeared:

AGNI: ("Reunion"); *Antioch Review*: ("In Lieu of an Ode"); *Artful Dodge*: ("Janus-Ingenuous"); *Crab Orchard Review*: ("The Difference"); *Cranky*: ("Cinqueterre," "La Strada Liggia"); *Cream City Review*: ("The Weather in Heaven"); *Gulf Coast*: ("Drowning Man"); *LitRag*: ("Gone West," "My Clone"); *The Mississippi Review*: ("An Olive," "Metal-liturgical"); *New Delta Review*: ("Steeplejack," "The Pantheon (1)"); *Ninth Letter*: ("Asceticism"); *The Plum Review*: ("Seastacks"); *Poetry*: ("Incense," "Toulouse," "Philology"); *Poetry Northwest*: ("Impressionism," "K," "Solar Prominence," "Sleeping Dogs"); *Pontoon 4*: ("Against Necessity"); *The Seattle Review*: ("Sopa de Pintas Negras," "Oysters"); *Southwest Review*: ("Umbrella Pines"); *32 Poems*: ("Two Ravens," "Birches"); *Verse*: ("To Err," "Can't Recant"); *Willow Springs*: ("Medical History"); *Wordwrights*: ("Baggage," "Café du Soleil," "Fin de Siècle" (as "Midi"))

"Janus-Ingenuous," "Incense," "To Err," and "Homebody" appear in *Contemporary Northwest Poets*, OSU/Ooligan Press, David Biespiel, Editor.
"Incense" was featured on *Poetry Daily*.
"Two Ravens" appeared as a limited edition broadside, published by Egress Studio Press.

"An Olive" is for Antonio Guerrero Gómez.
"Metal-liturgical" is for John Bisbee.
"Philology" is for Catherine Coan.

I am grateful for grants and fellowships awarded by the Bread Loaf Writers' Conference, the MacDowell Colony, the Bogliasco Foundation, the Camargo Foundation, and the Artist Trust of Washington State which helped this book into being.

I am also deeply indebted to friends and readers whose close and careful ministrations made it a better one: Michael Collier, Rod Jellema, Dan Lamberton, Carol Light, Heather McHugh, G.C. Waldrep, Kary Wayson, Andrew Zawacki. Thanks to Vern Rutsala, for finding my star among the many. And, *ad aperturam*, to R.K., for *urbanitas*, and grammar of the deepest kind and sense.

Author photo: Darren Darsey

ABOUT THE AUTHOR

Kevin Craft grew up in southern New Jersey and attended the University of Maryland where he received B.A.s in English and in French. He studied drama at the University of Sheffield in England, and later earned an M.F.A. in English from the University of Washington. His poems have appeared in many journals and reviews, including *Poetry, Verse, 9th Letter, AGNI,* and *Poetry Daily.* He currently resides in Seattle where he teaches English and writing at Everett Community College and for the University of Washington's Summer in Rome Seminar. A recipient of fellowships from the MacDowell Colony, the Bogliasco Foundation, the Camargo Foundation, and the Artist Trust of Washington State, he also directs the nascent Possession Sound Writers Conference in Everett, and is editor of the journal *Mare Nostrum.*

About the Publisher

Bedbug Press was founded in 1995 by Tony Gorsline, who has had a life-long love of books and writing. His inaugural publishing effort was *Going Over the Falls*, a collection of poetry, by Gretchen Sousa.

The name Cloudbank Books was established in 2000 by Peter Sears and Michael Malan with the publication of *Millennial Spring—Eight New Oregon Poets*.

Cloudbank Books became an imprint of Bedbug Press in 2002. Since that time, Bedbug Press has established, under its Cloudbank imprint, the Northwest Poetry Series and The Rhea & Seymour Gorsline Poetry Competition. In 2005, *Woman in the Water: A Memoir of Growing Up in Hollywood*, by Dorinda Clifton, was published by Bedbug Press. *Woman in the Water* is a creative non-fiction memoir. It is our hope that all of the Bedbug/Cloudbank books express our commitment to quality in writing and publishing.